THE 1960s HOME

Paul Evans

SHIRE PUBLICATIONS

SHIRE PUBLICATIONS
Bloomsbury Publishing Plc

Kemp House, Chawley Park, Oxford OX2 9PH, UK
29 Earlsfort Terrace, Dublin 2, Ireland
1385 Broadway, 5th Floor, New York, NY 10018, USA
Email: shire@bloomsbury.com
www.shirebooks.co.uk

SHIRE is a trademark of Osprey Publishing Ltd

First published in Great Britain in 2010
Transferred to digital print in 2015

Shire Library no. 604
Print ISBN: 978 0 74780 802 2
ePub: 978 0 74781 159 6
ePDF: 978 0 74780 991 3

Designed by Tony Truscott Designs, Sussex, UK
Typeset in Perpetua and Gill Sans
Printed and bound in India by Replika Press Private Ltd.

24 25 26 27   15 14 13 12 11 10 9

The Woodland Trust
Osprey Publishing supports the Woodland Trust, the UK's
leading woodland conservation charity.

www.shirebooks.co.uk
To find out more about our authors and books visit our
website. Here you will find extracts, author interviews,
details of forthcoming events and the option to sign-up
for our newsletter.

COVER IMAGE
Cover design by Peter Ashley. Front cover image:
Wallpaper by Sandersons, courtesy of Jane Clayton &
Company. Back cover detail: Tea storage jar by Hornsea
Pottery in the *Heirloom* design, collection PA.

TITLE PAGE IMAGE
Table setting with stainless steel accessories, 1962.

CONTENTS PAGE IMAGE
Textile wall hanging, late 1960s.

CONTENTS

INTRODUCTION

O F ALL the post-war decades, the 1960s have continued to fascinate subsequent generations above all others. Its fashions are endlessly revisited, its music revived and restyled and its home styles copied. For many the 1960s are also seen as a particularly 'British' decade – that of the Beatles, the Mini and the mini skirt, Twiggy and the 1966 World Cup. Of course the Swinging London of Carnaby Street would have seemed hopelessly remote to the majority of the British public at the time – yet the outward confidence of Britain in the 1960s did indeed have a profound effect on British society as a whole.

Although the British economy had failed to grow as spectacularly as that of some of its near neighbours during the late 1940s and 1950s, and the loss of Britain's imperial assets and prestige was at times a painful process, the period between 1945 and 1973 nevertheless saw sustained economic growth without major recession. That the then Prime Minister Harold MacMillan could famously state with some justification in 1957, 'most of our people have never had it so good', was evidence that British consumers were finally free of the long legacy of wartime exigencies and shortages. Yet MacMillan's famous statement contained also a warning of the threat that inflation posed during such a period of growth and increased consumption. Average wages between 1955 and 1960 rose by 34 per cent whilst the cost of many consumer items had, in real terms, fallen. Car ownership increased massively and the possession of a television or refrigerator – luxuries available to the privileged few in 1950 – had, by 1960, become the norm. The class divisions of British society, so marked in previous generations, had been greatly, although not entirely, eroded with the advent of universal state-funded education, and figures such as the Old Etonian MacMillan were increasingly seen as anachronisms, emblematic of pre-war institutional privilege. Increased social mobility and wealth encouraged far greater aspirations than previously, most markedly amongst young people, the 'baby boomer' generation born during and after the war.

British design had been one of the great hopes for post-war reconstruction as economists and planners argued that exportable, high-quality goods of superior design would help the British economy overcome its yawning trade deficit. The Britain Can Make It exhibition of 1946 and Festival of Britain of 1951 had sought to promote British design to overseas buyers, but, despite the quality of many British goods, by 1960 it was Scandinavia, Italy and the USA that led the world in design excellence, with the strong influence of Scandinavia becoming increasingly evident in British homes. The accepted conventions of most post-war design thinking were, however, to be consistently challenged through the 1960s. Fitness for purpose and honesty of materials were of course laudable aims and the general standard of manufactured goods for the home had never been higher, yet this was increasingly no longer enough to satisfy consumers – relatively wealthy by the standards of the 1940s and 1950s – for whom novelty and style were of equal importance to durability and functionality. This trend would become ever more apparent as the 1960s progressed. Above all other considerations though, it was the type and availability of housing that remained the paramount priority for most people.

A late 1960s 'country style' kitchen. This would be a popular style for many years to come.

DOMESTIC ARCHITECTURE

SOCIAL HOUSING

In 1960 the great majority of British housing stock had been built during the great housing booms of the late Victorian era and the inter-war period between 1918 and 1939. The Labour Government elected in 1945 had been faced with severe housing shortages caused by loss after bombing and by an increasing population. These problems were compounded by the poor and unsanitary condition of much Victorian housing fit only for demolition and clearance. The answer had been the widespread and intensive construction of new social housing, much of this in the form of flats and, as the 1950s progressed, tower blocks. Post-war urban planners saw high-density or high-rise tower blocks as the ideal solution to the problems of shortage, overcrowding and poor quality traditional terraced and back-to-back housing. Apartment buildings and tower blocks could be built far more economically than houses and used far less space, and the influential Parker Morris Report of 1961, *Homes for Tomorrow and Today*, lay down minimum standards of space and heating for social housing. Many tower block estates were built on inexpensive 'green field' sites on the outskirts of major cities, and tenants were lured with the promise of open spaces and fresh air (much traditional inner-city housing existed close to factories and industry with their resultant pollution). High-rise living also accorded well with the sympathies of many young architects employed by local authorities, graduates of universities and architectural schools firmly under the sway of prevailing modernist doctrine.

The building many looked to as the apotheosis of high-density urban dwelling was the Swiss architect Le Corbusier's Unité d'Habitation or *Cité Radieuse* apartment block in Marseilles, completed in 1952. With 337 apartments arranged over twelve floors complete with an internal shopping street and a children's nursery on the roof, *Cité Radieuse* would provide the intellectual blueprint and credentials for two decades of British social housing. Foremost amongst Le Corbusier's disciples in Britain were the controversial young architects Alison and Peter Smithson. Taking Le Corbusier's use of the

Opposite:
House in
Buckinghamshire,
Peter J. Aldington.

7

phrase *béton brut* to describe the rough cast concrete used at Unité d'Habitation they coined the term Brutalism (sometimes called New Brutalism) to describe their vision of modern architectural form. They believed that modern social housing should be built as 'streets in the sky' to replicate the sense of neighbourliness and belonging that many urban residents already felt in their traditional communities. The look of brutalist architecture was one of uncompromising, repetitive hard-edged geometry, most often using unpainted grey concrete as the primary material. The Smithsons themselves were not able to put into practice their ideas until the very end of the 1960s, with Robin Hood Gardens, a 213-flat council estate in Poplar, East London. However, their influence can be seen strongly already in 1961 with the opening in Sheffield of the

spectacular and at times notorious Park Hill Estate. Set on a hill close to Sheffield City centre and consisting of nearly 1,000 flats in blocks of between four and thirteen storeys and built on land cleared of slums, Park Hill dominates the Sheffield skyline. Its architects, Jack Lynn and Ivor Smith, were early exponents of deck access, essentially long open walkways onto which each apartment door opened, wide enough for a milk float to travel down, and named after cleared streets that had existed previously on the site. Despite the best intentions these 'streets in the sky' never managed to recreate the atmosphere of traditional city streets – whereas Le Corbusier

Opposite top:
Le Corbusier's
Unité d'Habitation,
Marseilles, 1952.

Opposite bottom:
Park Hill flats,
Sheffield, 1961,
contrasting with
the earlier
brickwork and
stonework in the
foreground.

Erno Goldfinger's
thirty-one storey
Trellick Tower in
West London,
finished in 1972,
still dominates its
surroundings and
is London's tallest
residential block.

9

had enclosed the streets in his Unité d'Habitation building, at Park Hill, raised on a hill in the chilly climes of South Yorkshire, they were left open to the elements. Park Hill, although structurally well built and initially popular with tenants, lapsed into steady decline through the 1970s and 1980s, beset with problems of crime and poor noise insulation. Controversially given an English Heritage Grade II listing in 1998 when many would rather have witnessed its demolition, Park Hill has recently begun major renovation.

Another landmark brutalist block, and similarly rehabilitated in recent years, is Erno Goldfinger's Trellick Tower in London's Westbourne Grove. Built between 1967 and 1972 and at thirty-one storeys the tallest residential tower block in London, Trellick Tower was effectively the sister building to the slightly smaller Balfron Tower of 1965 built in Poplar, East London. Both buildings, each dominating the sky-line of their respective East and West neighbourhoods, are distinctive for their slim profile and separate lift and service tower connected to the main tower at every third floor. The story of Trellick Tower in particular is extraordinary – built as something of a swansong in terms of high-rise housing, it rapidly developed an unsavoury reputation for crime and deprivation and became emblematic of what were considered to be the mistakes of 1960s planning. However, a shifting of fashion in the 1990s and the work of a dedicated residents' association has seen the re-appraised Trellick Tower recognised as one of London's most significant and iconic post-war buildings, listed in 1998, and now viewed as a chic and desirable address.

The problem of building high-density housing whilst retaining a semblance of the intimacy of traditional housing was convincingly resolved by the architect Neave Brown's blocks in Fleet

Terraced maisonettes and flats at Fleet Road, Neave Brown, 1967.

Road, North London, completed in 1967. Blending the materials and vocabulary of brutalism with that of a traditional London terrace, it provided split-level maisonettes and flats arranged in sets of two- and three-storey blocks with each dwelling afforded a private outdoor terrace or garden. Although a demonstrably effective approach, Fleet Road and other similar developments offer at best an adjunct to the main story of 1960s social housing, dwarfed as they are by the vast number (over 2,000 in London alone) of 'system-built' tower blocks built during this period and which can be seen on the outskirts of nearly all major British cities and towns. The constructional, not to mention social, problems associated with these blocks, which often used untried materials and techniques, was already becoming apparent by the end of the 1960s and the collapse in 1968 of one such block, Ronan Point in East London, marked the beginning of the end of the British experiment in high-rise housing.

System-built tower blocks in East London. These are typical of many such blocks built throughout the 1960s in most British towns and cities.

PRIVATE HOUSING

Throughout the 1950s the Government had been the biggest client for house builders as post-war reconstruction got under way – such was the public sector need for materials and manpower that private house-building had been

Right and below:
Townhouses were
a popular style
throughout the
1960s.

heavily restricted until 1954. By 1960, however, the balance had tipped in favour of the private sector, a trend that has continued ever since. Much 1960s domestic housing is marked by a simplicity of style with large front picture windows, sometimes double glazed, flush exterior doors and shallow

pitched roofs. Occasionally concrete panels were used with brick to add textural variety to frontages; likewise rough-hewn stone walls were juxtaposed with brick, a technique pioneered by the Bauhaus-trained architect Marcel Breuer in the 1940s and 1950s.

A house style that enjoyed a marked revival in the 1960s was the terraced townhouse. Georgian townhouses had for some years been championed by architectural critics as exemplary urban housing and

Houses by the
architect Mervyn
Seal – a 1963
newspaper article
described them as
'the exotic
butterflies of
Devon'.

Right and below: Suburban low-rise flats. The rectilinear style and large windows are features common to many blocks built in the 1960s.

their elegant, simple style, combined with economical use of land – when real estate prices everywhere were rising – saw their updated 1960s counterparts built in numbers throughout Britain. Usually flat roofed and set over three, sometimes four, floors, many used part of the ground floor

as an integral garage, with living room and kitchen placed on the first floor and bedrooms above. Kitchens and living rooms were frequently built open plan, with the light from large, sometimes full height, windows increasing the sense of space and airiness. Ceilings conversely were usually slightly lower than in previous decades and outdoor space often limited to small front and back yards – this aspect in particular reflecting the belief at the time that young couples with children would not want the responsibility of maintaining gardens.

One manifestation of the buoyant economy of the 1960s was the number of showpiece, individually designed houses that were built. The spectacular private houses designed by the West Country architect Mervyn Seal with their signature 'butterfly' roofs are some of the finest examples. In a style reminiscent of Frank Lloyd Wright's Fallingwater, Seal's Parkham Wood House cantilevers dramatically over a cliff face above the Devon fishing town of Brixham, its master bedroom projecting out above the main room to provide uninterrupted views to the sea. The housing work of the young architect Peter Aldington drew comparison with that of the renowned Finnish architect Alvar Aalto, and his three houses built in Haddenham, Buckinghamshire between 1964 and 1968, Turn End, Middle Turn and The Turn showed how modern architecture and landscaping could successfully exist in a historic village setting.

Modern apartment blocks appeared in the suburbs of many towns. Typically these were brick built and no more than four or five storeys high, with upper floors having full-height windows and top floors often designated as spacious penthouse apartments. Wooden cladding or tiles were often used to interrupt the repetitive pattern characteristic of bare brick. At the same time as many new apartment buildings were being built a great number of larger older houses, built in an age when a house might need to accommodate both a large family and domestic staff, were subdivided into flats.

Not all sectors of society subscribed to the attractions of living in modern houses and flats and the early 1960s witnessed a growing trend amongst the professional middle classes to seek out properties in what had been traditionally working class inner-city areas, particularly in London. The sociologist Ruth Glass, working at the University of London, first described this phenomenon as 'gentrification' in a 1964 study of the north London district of Barnsbury. Early gentrifiers were attracted to the large and characterful yet inexpensive period properties available in down-at-heel areas such as Notting Hill and Islington, with their easy access to the attractions and nightlife of central London. As middle-class householders were moving into these areas many of the existing working-class communities were drifting towards the suburbs and beyond, often following the light industries which had employed them.

INTERIORS

D ESPITE the boom in house building in the years since 1945, most people still lived in properties built before the war, which, by the 1960s, may have been seen as outdated by their occupants. The fashion for 'do it yourself' first seen in the 1940s and 1950s and originally a reaction to post-war exigencies, continued to burgeon, with an emphasis on modernisation. A typical project might be the removal of a traditional cast-iron Victorian tiled fireplace or the facing of a Georgian panelled door with flush plywood. Again the ornate cornicing and ceiling mouldings characteristic of Victorian and earlier properties were often removed or replaced with shallower and simpler designs.

Such modifications apart, it was the choices householders in both new and old properties made in furniture and colour schemes that would have the greatest effect on the style of their homes.

FURNITURE
By 1960 the spindly, whimsical styles so characteristic of much 1950s furniture, influenced as it had been by the New Look and the Atomic Age, had largely been superseded by more formally functional rectilinear styles as well as by the fashion for Scandinavian, particularly Danish, furniture, with teak and occasionally the more luxurious rosewood as the principal materials used. Appreciation of Scandinavian furniture and design had its roots as far back as the 1930s, in select circles at least, but it was the work of the post-war generation of designers that impressed itself most firmly on British homes. From the mid-1950s Scandinavian design was illustrated extensively in home magazines. Whilst the British buying public may have admired the elegant forms and craftsmanship of the new Danish furniture its principal drawback was its high cost and its availability through relatively few retailers. Nevertheless as incomes rose in the late 1950s and early 1960s the market for this furniture increased, at least amongst the more affluent middle classes, and was catered for by specialist boutique furniture shops such as Scandia and Finmar. Teak dining room suites from Denmark were popular above all,

Opposite:
This 1966 setting shows the trend towards pale woods and bright colours.

Interior with
Danish furniture,
early 1960s.

G-Plan 'Danish
Line' dining suite
designed by Ib
Kofod-Larsen.

a typical style being the extendable dining table with matching chairs – sometimes with cane or leather upholstered seats – and a long sideboard with drawers and sliding doors. This style of furniture was usually given a simple oil finish producing a low but lustrous finish, in marked contrast to the heavily French-polished furniture of previous generations. Danish modern lounge chairs and settees were usually minimally upholstered and held in sculptural teak frames and raised on gently tapering legs. Not all Scandinavian furniture was so restrained though – the famous Egg and Swan chairs designed by Arne Jacobsen and Verner Panton's futuristic Cone chair appeared in the last two years of the 1950s and began to be offered to British customers in the early 1960s.

British manufacturers catering for the mass market closely followed the vogue for Scandinavian furniture and began to market their own designs in the 'Scandinavian style', but these were available at less prohibitive cost than the imported (and heavily taxed) originals. Most prominent amongst them was the High Wycombe manufacturer E. Gomme with their G-Plan range. G-Plan had existed since 1952 producing well made, if somewhat uninspired and derivative, furniture in the so-called 'Contemporary' style including Scandinavian influenced ranges. Conscious of losing sales to imported furniture in the early 1960s they contracted the talented Danish designer Ib Kofod-Larsen to design a 'Danish Line' range of furniture to be made in England. Bearing the stamp 'G-Plan Danish Design' with facsimile Kofod-Larsen signature the range consisted of living room, dining and bedroom furniture, mostly of teak construction, accented with rosewood handles. The range was a commercial success and was augmented by other Kofod-Larsen designs until the end of the decade. G-Plan's position as a leading manufacturer of modern furniture was consolidated with the launch of their hugely successful

**G-Plan have designs on Samantha
(Designs on Evlan and Courtelle too!)**

SCANDINAVIAN **DESIGN**
BY **NATHAN**

FURNITURE BY NATHAN

Fresco range in 1967 – still showing a clear Scandinavian influence. Hugely successful, some of the original Fresco range is still manufactured today.

Gomme's G-Plan range was hardly alone in treading the path of Scandinavian sourced style, and many manufacturers by the early 1960s had their own ranges which, if not actually designed in Denmark, borrowed heavily from its look. One British company, Nathan, advertised its range as 'Scandinavian Design by Nathan' and alongside G-Plan and Nathan, companies such as Meredew, Younger and McIntosh competed for the booming middle market, with stylistically safe modern ranges, the models often combining solid and veneered woods. Not all lived up to Danish levels of quality and craftsmanship, with teak-effect plastic veneers appearing on some lamentable ranges available at the cheapest end of the market.

A British company that followed a somewhat different approach was the High Wycombe maker Ercol, whose designs had first been seen shortly after the war. Their furniture was rooted in traditional English country styles and materials, particularly yew wood, yet still imbued with a strong sense of the modern. Popular offerings in the Ercol range included their Windsor chairs and rockers, room dividers and sideboards, and sets of nesting pebble-shaped coffee tables. An aesthetic if not overly commercial success was a low slung lounge or TV chair offered in the early 1960s available with or without arms.

The Nottingham company Stag enjoyed the services of the talented designers John and Sylvia Reid whose 'C' range of starkly modernist

Above left: Affordable yet modern – late 1960s advertisement for G-Plan's Samantha and Fresco ranges.

Above: Many British furniture manufacturers marketed their own Scandinavian-style furniture.

bedroom furniture had been a surprise commercial success in the 1950s. Looking perhaps more to America than Scandinavia for inspiration, their teak and metal dining room furniture was a tour de force of early 1960s British design. Equally distinctive was their Fineline range of bedroom furniture, which used pale birch veneers cut end on and finished with aluminium legs and handles. Such was the Reids' flexibility, however, that their greatest success for Stag was distinctly revivalist – their Minstrel series of living and bedroom furniture, launched in 1964, was an eighteenth-century-inspired (though still

Ercol's elm and beech furniture offered an alternative to the teak used by many manufacturers.

minstrel is not for everyone. Only for those who welcome the classical lines and lustrous surface that echo the Golden Age of English furniture design. Finished in cherry mahogany and lined throughout in mahogany veneer, Minstrel slips elegantly into the scheme of things. Its looks, too, are matched by the Stag quality of its construction, by the practical usefulness of every item in the range and, not least, by prices which represent unbeatable value for money.

THE STAG CABINET CO. LTD. (UK) HAYDN ROAD, NOTTINGHAM

Name

Address

STAG

functional) range. Equally unafraid of risk was the firm of L. Lazarus who marketed their furniture as Uniflex and whose ranges included melamine-faced unit furniture and some highly distinctive teak and rosewood cabinets and sideboards designed by Peter Hayward.

The top end of the domestic furniture market was well contested by British manufacturers. Competing against each other as well as against foreign imports for market share, many of these companies recognised that design excellence was paramount in winning over an increasingly discerning clientele. Heals of Tottenham Court Road remained the leading retailer of high quality contemporary furniture, selling imported Scandinavian, Italian and American designs as well as its own ranges, including pieces designed by Robert Heritage and manufactured by Archie Shine. The Cotswold firm of

Above left: Stag's Fineline range was highly modern …

… but its revivalist Minstrel range (above) was a better seller.

Teak and rosewood cabinet designed by Peter Hayward for Uniflex.

Gordon Russell continued its tradition of producing beautifully crafted and restrained modern furniture using exotic hardwoods. Much of the Russell output was aimed at the export and contract market, as was that of the East London company Hille & Co, although both retained a domestic presence.

The 1950s work of Hille's designer Robin Day had been widely admired and influential — a rare instance at the time of a British designer with a truly international reputation. His 1960s work is most famous for his hugely successful

Chair by William
Plunkett, 1967.

(over 20 million sold) polypropylene stacking chairs launched in 1963. Many of Day's other designs from the 1960s are strongly rectilinear and geometric,

Harrods room set
with Danish
furniture, from
1963.

especially his glass and steel Alpha tables of 1959 and his luxurious afrormosia, chromed steel and leather Forum armchair and settee of 1962.

Even more committed to a hard-edged modern aesthetic was William Plunkett who eschewed the use of wood entirely in the designs he produced for his company William Plunkett Ltd, established in 1963. His Reigate rocking chair of 1963 used a

Swivelling lounge chairs were a new and popular form.

The Ladderax shelving system offered stylish and flexible storage for homeowners.

Cardboard chair designed by Peter Murdoch in 1963.

Eero Aarnio's Ball chair made a strong statement but found favour in only a few homes.

frame of simple flat steel finished in grey nylon with thin, removable, foam-filled cushions. Similarly his Coulsden coffee table used a chrome steel platform and heavy glass top.

In addition to Robin Day's designs Hille began to produce, under licence, those of the American designer Charles Eames in 1962, including his world famous 670 Lounge chair. The masculine appeal of the well-upholstered swivelling lounge chair was a form that many designers would visit during the 1960s with efforts ranging from the egg-like Revolvers range of Greaves & Thomas through G-Plan's swivelling wing chairs to Robin Day's angular black leather and steel Leo chair from 1965.

Storage, then as now, was often a problem and a popular solution first seen in the early 1960s were flexible shelving and storage systems, which could also serve as room dividers. Especially popular in Britain was the Ladderax system designed by Robert Heal and manufactured by Staples & Co Ltd. Ladderax used white or black enamelled steel uprights, or ladders, upon which shelves or units – usually teak veneered – could be hung. With ladders available in five heights and shelves in five widths a wide variety of arrangements was possible. Similar systems were marketed by Remploy and Brianco.

Towards the middle of the decade the ubiquity of tasteful Scandinavian-influenced furniture had begun to be challenged by younger British and Continental designers interested in new materials and forms. Partially this was a reaction against prevalent modernist design orthodoxy and partially an attempt to produce design that appealed most of all to the young. Maxima, a range of knock-down, white painted plywood furniture designed by the young Northern Irish designer Max Clendinning was made briefly by Race Furniture in 1965, and at around the same time a range of flat-packed cardboard chairs printed with large polka dots designed by Peter Murdoch appeared. The significance today of these experiments is more that they were emblematic of the confidence and daring of mid-Sixties 'pop' culture than any effect they had on mainstream furniture-buying habits, where the influence of pop aesthetics was largely confined to upholstery textiles. A surprising commercial success though was the Tomotom range of brightly painted cylindrical chairs and tables made of compressed paper and designed by Bernard Holdaway for Hull Traders Ltd in 1966.

Of more lasting significance than paper chairs and tables was the plastic furniture, particularly from Italy, that began to appear at the end of the decade, which made a bright, if limited, addition to some adventurous interiors. Amongst the better-selling designs were the stacking Universale and Selene chairs designed by Joe Colombo and Vico Magistretti respectively. Perhaps the most famous example of 1960s plastic furniture was the Finnish designer Eero Aarnio's Ball Chair, which was seen in both the popular TV series *The Prisoner* and the film *The Italian Job*. It sold in tiny quantities as much because of its high price as its size, being too big to pass through most domestic door frames.

By the late 1960s tastes were beginning to drift away from avowedly modern styles with a commensurate revival of interest in the styles of the Victorian era and to a lesser extent that of the 1930s. Young urban home-makers were as likely to scour antique and junk shops for furniture as they were to visit a department store. Purchases might include a pine Welsh dresser or kitchen table or a traditional spindle-backed Windsor chair. Often these could be made to work well in informal settings with more modern furniture. The major retrospective Bauhaus Exhibition held at the Royal Academy in the Summer of 1968 provoked renewed interest in the chromed tubular steel furniture of the pre-war years. A particular favourite design, in a re-edition by the American company Knoll, was Marcel Breuer's landmark leather and chrome Wassily chair, first produced in 1928. Such historicism would become a distinguishing feature of homes throughout the 1970s.

LIGHTING

The exuberance of much 1950s lighting – characterised by asymmetry, hourglass shades, bright colours and etiolated brass stems – was still in evidence in many designs available to the householder at the start of the 1960s. These styles however, which owed much to Italian lighting design, were being challenged by the

Danish table lamp and floor lamp from the early 1960s – teak and brass were popular materials.

Aluminium was used to achieve a sharp and engineered look – desk lamp by Gerald Abramovitz for Best & Lloyd.

coolly rational lighting forms arriving from Scandinavia, with the PH ceiling lights of veteran Danish designer Poul Henningsen promoted as archetypes of good lighting design. These featured symmetrical graduating louvres aimed at diffusing light evenly and avoiding harshness.

Henningsen's designs and ideas were widely adopted in much 1960s lighting, particularly by other Scandinavian manufacturers such as Fog & Morup and Lyfa whose designs were sold widely throughout the decade. Danish style can also be seen in the teak and brass table- and standard lamps offered by many retailers.

Teardrop glass shade made in Denmark.

These simple shades used brightly coloured plastic inserts to provide interesting optical effects. John and Sylvia Reid for Rotaflex, early 1960s.

Effective lighting design also exercised the creative talents of some of Britain's best industrial designers. John and Sylvia Reid, noted for their furniture designs for Stag, were also consultant designers for the lighting manufacturers Rotaflex. Their Metallux range, designed between 1958 and 1962, featured wall, ceiling, floor and table lamps using innovative light-dispersing, perforated shades while other models featured brightly coloured plastic inserts set into cylindrical metal shades. Popular task lights included the evergreen Anglepoise lamps, little changed since the 1930s, and the quirky Maclamps with their painted shades and wooden arms, which sold through Habitat and by mail order. Uncompromisingly modern was the range of desk lamps designed by Gerald Abramovitz for Best & Lloyd in 1962. Best & Lloyd already enjoyed a tradition of producing modernist lighting, principally its Bestlite table lamp introduced in 1933. Abramovitz's stark design featured a cantilevered aluminium shade housing a fluorescent tube raised on a narrow stem and box-shaped housing for switch and transformer.

Perhaps in keeping with its brutalist sensitivities it was given a number (41555 Mark 2) rather than a name. It remains one of the most

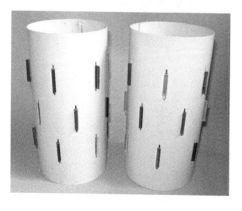

startling lamp designs of the 1960s, despite its short production run. The range of minimalist aluminium table- and floor lamps introduced by Peter Nelson's company Architectural Lighting Ltd in 1962 shared much of 41555 Mark 2's stark, engineered aesthetic. They sold relatively well though and were widely imitated throughout the decade. Aluminium was also the material of choice in many of the ceiling- and wall-mounted spotlight systems that appeared in the second half of the decade, with some models using tracked systems for maximum flexibility.

For those preferring a somewhat softer and less masculine look a wide range of glass fittings was available. Typical designs would be simple teardrop-shaped pendants made of either opaque white or cased coloured glass.

Above left: Glass and aluminium Conelight fitting, 1967.

Above right: Lumitron table lamp designed by Robert Welch, 1966. This range used smoked acrylic shades on elegant tulip-shaped bases.

Originally available by mail order, the Maclamp later became a bestseller for Habitat.

27

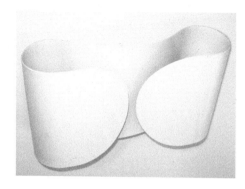

Foglio wall lamp by
Tobia Scarpa, 1966.

Designs from the Danish glass manufacturers Holmegaard were particularly popular, as were the more flamboyant versions arriving from Italy. Home- produced versions also sold well and an attractive blend of aluminium and glass can be seen in the simple wall lights produced around 1967 by the English company Conelight and designed by E. Cooke Yarborough.

Lighting could be fun too and the late 1960s saw the arrival of such novelties as the first lava lamps, invented by the Englishman Edward Craven Walker in 1963. These contained a mixture of oil and coloured wax held in a glass container, which would, when warmed by a lightbulb, cause the illuminated blob of wax to constantly shift and alter its shape. Other fun offerings included the brightly coloured table lamps of solid cast resin matched with orange fibreglass shades sold widely by British Home Stores. Hanging shades printed with flowery pop art or psychedelic motifs were widely available, whilst Habitat stores likewise offered brightly enamelled pendants as well as flat-packed shades that produced striking geometric arrangements when assembled.

Late-1960s lighting is notable in particular for its increased use of plastics. Bakelite had been used in lighting since the 1930s but its widespread use had been compromised by its brittleness and tendency to crack when hot or handled carelessly. Advances in materials and moulding technology allowed, by the 1960s, plastic lighting to be produced in forms limited only by designers' imagination. Clear or tinted plastic, employed where glass might once have been used, feature in many designs, notably Robert Welch's Lumitron range from 1966, which used blue-tinted acrylic dome shades set on anodised aluminium bases. Many designs using plastic came from Italy

Candleholders
were popular and
came in many
styles.

and included such designs as Vico Magistretti's simple organic Dalu table lamp of 1966 and Joe Colombo's lamps for Kartell. Stylish as such products were they nevertheless sold in quite small quantities, with the British public yet to accept such overtly plastic products into their living rooms.

ACCESSORIES

The sleek lines of many 1960s interiors discouraged clutter and favoured a sparing use of ornamentation, with bolder and larger – but fewer – pieces of decorative pottery and glass preferred. Nevertheless, most householders would choose carefully from a range of accessories that would lend individuality to living rooms and dining tables. Organic, sculptural teak bowls from Denmark were popular as were small abstract sculptures in wood, metal or marble. Candles were ever popular and often used as an antidote to sometimes harsh, though highly efficient, modern electric lighting. Whereas the bohemian householder of 1969 might prefer a plain candle in the neck of an empty wine bottle his counterpart of five or ten years before would prefer one of the many elegant candleholders available. As always, Scandinavian designs sold well, with varieties in teak, pottery, silver-plate and cast iron all popular. Robert Welch's heavy cast-iron candleholders, finished in rough matt black enamel, reflected the increased use of texture seen in many areas of domestic design.

Other decorative touches included a growing fondness for small Victorian antiques – the quirkier the better – with vintage globes and model sailing ships both particularly prized. Such trends would be become more pronounced by the beginning of the 1970s as styles became increasingly eclectic and ready to embrace the fashions and material culture of previous generations.

HOME ENTERTAINMENT

The impact of television on British homes, particularly in the second half of the 1950s, had been profound and by the early 1960s most households contained a television set, with daily life increasingly oriented towards TV viewing. The purchase of a television represented a significant financial commitment for most families, and many sets were either rented or bought using hire purchase. Broadcast output was still quite limited in 1960 although the launch of ITV in 1955 meant that there was at least some choice. BBC 2 began broadcasting in 1964, using a higher frequency than the existing two channels and necessitating expensive set conversions for those determined to enjoy the new channel. Colour television arrived in 1967 although few

Teak-framed mirror made by G-Plan, mid-1960s.

The compact size of many 1960s television sets meant that they were ideal for placing in room dividers and storage units.

programmes were broadcast in colour and most people only had black-and-white sets. Improvements in tube and transistor technology meant that the television sets of the 1960s were much less bulky and more reliable, with better picture quality than their 1950s forebears. Most television sets were still British made with manufacturers such as Pye, Ferguson and Bush the market leaders. Although the advent of television had a big impact on British homes the sets themselves were largely unassuming, typically housed in simple teak or mahogany veneered cabinets with control panels of plastic or brushed aluminium. A marked exception to the conservatism of most television set design was the space-age-inspired Keracolor Sphere set designed by Arthur Bracegirdle in 1968.

As the television set supplanted the heavy static family wireless radio set in most homes, so radios became smaller and more portable, aided again by advances in transistor technology. In the 1950s British radio manufacturers had looked towards America for styling direction but by the early 1960s a more minimalist, rectilinear approach was becoming evident. Clearly showing the influence of the German designer Dieter Rams, whose radio designs for Braun had been widely published in *Design* magazine, the Rio range of portable transistor radios was launched to acclaim by the British company Ultra in 1961. Designed by Eric Marshall, Rio combined slim plastic cases in subdued pastel colours with large easy-to-read dials and chunky push button controls. The range won the prestigious Duke of Edinburgh's Award for Elegant Design in 1961.

Elegant too were the radios and audio equipment produced by the Danish manufacturer Bang & Olufsen, which developed a strong following amongst well-heeled British audiophiles in the 1960s. Their Beolit range of portable transistor radios were distinctive for their sleek teak cabinets and

sophisticated circuitry. The technologically advanced Beolit 800 model from 1965 featured an ingenious system whereby extra 'feet' would pop out of its cabinet allowing it to be placed on its side without fear of being damaged or marked. A more affordable rival to Bang & Olufsen was the British company Roberts, whose radios, with a reputation for quality and durability if not cutting-edge design, were consistently bestsellers in a market under considerable pressure from Far Eastern imports.

Popular music in the late 1950s and early 1960s was largely driven by sales of 45rpm singles and the equipment used to play them was accordingly basic, with combined record player and speaker combinations of the Dansette variety a popular choice. With increasingly sophisticated multi-track stereo recording techniques and the growth in popularity of long playing (LP) records in the mid-1960s came greater demand for high-quality audio equipment. Cased radiograms containing record player and speakers catered for most needs but for true enthusiasts a Hi-Fi system with separate turntable, amplifier and speakers was the only option. Initially this market was catered for by specialist British manufacturers such as Leak and Garrard, but as the market grew so did competition from Japanese manufacturers.

Radios by Ultra, Bang & Olufsen and Roberts.

WALLS
Most manufacturers concentrated on producing traditional style wallpapers for the mass market, whilst the tendency in fashionable modern settings was for white and cream sometimes counterpointed with pale colours including

muted blues, greens and pinks. Walls or even
ceilings of tongue and groove in pine or
other pale wood could be seen in some
homes – a device first popularised by
Scandinavian designers. A popular and
effective means of achieving texture for
interior walls was the use of bare or
whitewashed brick – this had been a
favoured device of modernist architects for
some time, notably in Aalto's Villa Mairea of
1940 and in many of the influential
Californian Case Study Houses built after
the war.

Pictures and paintings were often the
chief means of adding interest to wall space
– naturally bold abstract expressionist works
were in evidence although a favourite and
effective device of some interior designers
of the period was to include jarringly
anachronistic paintings from previous
centuries, often in heavy gilt frames, in otherwise coolly modernist room
settings. Textile wall hangings were also popular, with French and
Scandinavian imports as well as British designs seen in many homes. Warmer,
darker colours – yellows, oranges and blues were in use by the mid-1960s,
anticipating the use of even stronger colours by the end of the decade. The
late 1960s also saw a resurgence in the use of wallpapers – hessian papers
were popular and some bold colourful floral or psychedelic designs appeared,
often aimed at the youthful, first home market. Other patterns took their
lead from the op art movement pioneered by Bridget Riley and Victor
Vasarely. A growing interest in Victorian and Art Nouveau styles in the last
years of the decade saw some 70- and 80-year-old patterns revived, whilst
reproductions of *fin de siècle* posters by the likes of Toulouse Lautrec and
Alphonse Mucha adorned many walls.

Wallpaper design
with op art
influence.

FLOORING

Developments and improvements in the production of man-made fibres
made fitted wall-to-wall carpets both practical and affordable. Styles available
at the beginning of the decade ranged from plain colours or traditional floral
chintzes through to abstract patterns. Initially these abstract designs were
offered in quite muted colour-ways but as the decade progressed
manufacturers were offering increasingly bold and colourful patterns, at least
for living room carpets where strong patterns had the advantage of

Opposite:
Hi-Fi equipment
came into many
homes during the
1960s – these
Bang & Olufsen
components would
have been highly
desirable and share
this room setting
with other Danish
designs.

A strongly geometric carpet design from 1963, seen with 'Shaftesbury' teak storage unit and with chairs by Peter Hoyte (foreground) and Robin Day.

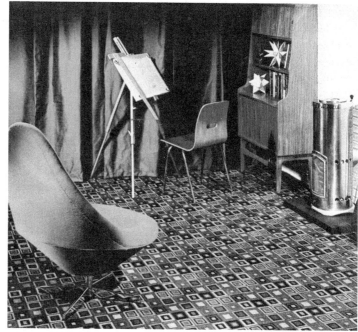

Scandinavian Rya rug.

concealing dirt and marks. Bedroom carpets tended towards the plain, pale and neutral.

In newly built houses and flats with concrete sub-floors, wooden block flooring was often used, typically using smaller blocks of light coloured wood in contrast to the familiar herringbone pattern parquet used in many pre-war properties. If these floors were not carpeted over then rugs were often used to provide texture and warmth. A particularly popular style was the Scandinavian Rya rug – these were characterised by their bold abstract designs and strong colours with deep shades of orange and red often used. Alternatives to the Rya might be a traditional Persian Kilim, increasingly popular through the decade and into the 1970s, or inexpensive plain floor coverings of natural materials such as jute or sea grass. First seen in American homes, the long-haired woollen white shag pile rug was seen as a particularly glamorous choice.

HEATING

Central heating was a luxury found in very few older homes at the start of the decade with most households still reliant on open fireplaces. However, the growing availability of affordable electric or more often gas-fired boilers meant that the inclusion of thermostatically controlled central heating was a practical, if major, investment for householders. Testament to this are the many advertisements for boilers found in newspapers and interior design magazines from the period. Simple panel radiators were preferred to the bulky versions of pre-war years – one system even channelled heat through skirting boards – and if fireplaces were retained at all they would often house only a simple gas fire. A 1961 catalogue of fireplaces available from the furnishers Heals shows a number of designs using materials as diverse as marble, slate, wood and stainless steel. A common feature of all is their slim profile and lack of applied ornamentation. For those without full central heating, portable oil-filled or electric convection heaters were marketed widely. As domestic heating systems improved so too did insulation and double glazing began to appear in new homes and as a replacement option in older properties.

Above; Central heating systems were widely advertised.

Catalogue of fireplace designs from Heals, 1961.

TEXTILES

IF BRITAIN lagged behind Italy, Scandinavia and the USA in many fields of design during the 1950s this could not be said of its contribution to textile design. The energy and innovation seen in the work of designers such as Lucienne Day, Marian Mahler and Jacqueline Groag and manufacturers David Whitehead and Edinburgh Weavers established Britain as world leaders in this field. In common with other trends at the beginning of the 1960s the spiky and atomic-age-inspired designs of the 1950s were evolving into simpler linear motifs. Emphasis was also placed on the textural qualities of fabrics, with the use of open weaves and coarser threads. Earthy colours predominated, typically browns, greens and pale blues. The medium of textile design is naturally subject to the influence of the fine arts, particularly painting, and a number of designs were commissioned from leading artists. Many such designs, often uncompromising and 'difficult' found a more ready market in corporate rather than domestic environments. A notable exception was 'Stones of Bath', commissioned by Sanderson of the painter and printmaker John Piper in 1959 and issued in 1962. At the forefront of British abstract painting before the war, Piper's style had become increasingly romantic, with his many representations of English country churches and landscapes. Neither wholly abstract nor entirely representational, with its submerged glimpses of archaic arches under blocks of jewel-like colour, Stones of Bath was a significant, if surprising, commercial bestseller. The success of Piper's design was partly that it worked well when seen in large expanses, as when used as floor-to-ceiling curtains; such arrangements were becoming increasingly commonplace with the abundant fenestration that was a defining characteristic of 1960s domestic architecture. Patterns with much larger repeats than had been seen before, which might once have seemed disproportionately bold when used on traditionally sized windows, became widely fashionable. Geometric and Op-Art influenced as well as floral patterns with oversized repeats were produced by a number of manufacturers. Op-Art pioneer Victor Vasarely produced designs for Edinburgh Weavers but it was Barbara Brown's designs for Heals that

Opposite:
The influence of Art Deco can be seen in this late-1960s Sanderson pattern, Bye-bye Blackbird, by Robert Holmes.

Above: Stones of Bath textile by John Piper for Sanderson.

Above right: Pattern repeats were both bold and large.

managed to combine critical acclaim with buoyant sales. Brown began selling her designs to Heals even before graduating from the Royal College of Art in 1956 and produced designs for them throughout the decade, becoming known as 'Heals' Golden Girl' — such was her ability to come up with consistently bankable designs. Her strongly geometric Reciprocation and Recurrence fabrics from 1962 used contrasting arrangements of squares and discs (Recurrence was adapted for use by Midwinter on their Focus range of tableware) whilst Complex from 1967 used contrasting light and shade to achieve a remarkable sense of depth. A design from 1969, Frequency, with its rolling bands of graduating colour, was inspired by radio waves as seen on a screen and embodies much of the spirit of late-1960s pattern design. Brown's work shares an affinity with that of her contemporary, Shirley Craven, working at Hull Traders, who produced a great number of typically abstract organic designs.

In addition to the sort of monumental abstract designs produced by Brown and Craven, floral designs were enormously popular, particularly from the middle of the decade onwards. Often these were stylised and heavily simplified, reductivist designs in bold colours and set in linear arrangements. Such designs were an early staple of Habitat's range of fabrics aimed at the younger shoppers setting up home.

The Art Nouveau and Art Deco revivals at the end of the decade were evident in a number of designs – sometimes as re-editions of Victorian designs (occasionally produced in more up-to-date colour schemes) or as pastiches of earlier styles. Robert Holmes' giddy art-deco-style Bye-bye Blackbird fabric for Sanderson was a notable example. In marked contrast to such designs the late 1960s also saw increasing use of plain venetian and roller blinds in domestic interiors, although occasionally these too would feature printed designs.

Sunrise fabric by Lucienne Day, 1969.

Below left and right: Two fabric designs for Heals – Recurrence fabric seen in the contemporary room set, and Complex from 1967 (below).

POTTERY AND GLASS

POTTERY

British pottery manufacturers had enjoyed relatively prosperous times during the 1950s; even imported Scandinavian designs, lauded by the design establishment and widely illustrated in style magazines, had failed to seriously threaten their market dominance. The industry was, however, marked by an over-proliferation of manufacturers, which on the one hand encouraged innovation but on the other made smaller companies especially prone to market fluctuations, and the 1960s witnessed a gradual thinning of the industry as the major manufacturers absorbed their smaller competitors. Most contemporary tableware was transfer printed by 1960, although hand-painted designs were still available. While Woolworths still stocked that most iconic 1950s design, Ridgway's Homemaker, well into the middle of the decade, the whimsicality of many 1950s patterns was gradually replaced by more linear motifs used on taller, cylindrical shapes. The busy geometric designs of Kathie Winkle's work for James Broadhurst are particularly illustrative of this trend. The Burslem company of W. R. Midwinter was one of the most progressive manufacturers of tableware throughout the 1950s and early 1960s, and abstract patterns such as Sienna from 1962, the Op-Art-inspired Focus of 1964 and Mexicana from 1966 were artistic and commercial successes. Other, later, Midwinter patterns reliant on stylised floral and Eastern motifs were commercial failures and the company was taken over by a competitor, J. & G. Meakin in 1968. It was symptomatic of the pottery industry that even well-established and hitherto successful companies could fail on the strength of a few unpopular designs, but two small companies that bucked this trend were Hornsea and Portmeirion. The small family company of Hornsea was established only a few years after the war but its innovative products, typically with matt white glazed bodies with impressed linear or geometric designs filled with pastel colours, had been an instant hit with style-conscious buyers. Early successes were bolstered by the launch of their Heirloom range in 1967, which featured a lightly textured repeat crystal-like pattern in matt black glaze applied over brown, green or

Opposite:
Italian glass
decanters by Toso,
1961.

41

Above: Viscount, a typically colourful design by Kathie Winkle for James Broadhurst.

Above right: Midwinter Mexicana pattern, 1966.

Below and right: Bestsellers: Denby's Arabesque and Hornsea's Heirloom.

Arabesque is made by Denby in audaciously different shapes and all conquering colours...attractive aesthetic, and...

oven-to-table practical!

dark blue body colours. A favourite on many newlyweds'
wedding lists, it vied only with Denby's Arabesque pattern
dinnerware in popularity.

Texture was also a key feature in the coffee sets
designed by Susan Williams-Ellis for her company
Portmeirion Potteries Ltd, named after the fantastic
Italianate village in North Wales designed by her father
between 1925 and 1975. Her Totem range of 1963 – the
company having been founded in 1962 – featured very tall
cylindrical coffee pots with embossed abstract symbols.
Totem was followed by other radical designs including the
wildly abstract Variations line of 1964 (with a coffee pot
adorned with an extravagant scimitar-shaped handle) and
the bestselling Magic City of 1966.

The success of Portmeirion's quirky designs may have
provided some of the motivation behind Royal Worcester's
decision to commission the 'outsider' artist Scottie Wilson
– who counted Picasso amongst his many admirers – to transfer his
mystical visions onto a range of tableware and coffee sets launched
in 1966.

Imported alternatives to British ranges largely came from
Scandinavia. Though relatively expensive the Finnish company
Arabia's sophisticated Ruska tableware, designed by Ulla Procope in
1960, was consistently popular and sold through up-market retailers such as
Heals. The subtleties of hue found in its deep brown glaze lent it a hand-
made quality unusual in an age of standardised mass production. It also had
the advantage of being ovenproof when few of its competitors were.

Interest in craft and studio pottery gained considerable momentum
during the later 1960s and into the 1970s with a proliferation of small

Magic City coffee
pot, Susan
Williams-Ellis.
Portmeirion
Potteries Ltd,
1966.

Tableware
designed by the
'outsider' artist
Scottie Wilson for
Royal Worcester,
1967.

43

Ruska service by
Ulla Procope for
Arabia, 1960.

Cornish Troika
'wheel' vase from
the late 1960s.

potteries based in rural locations and dependent upon the tourist trade. Much output was in styles derivative of pioneer studio potters such as Bernard Leach and Michael Cardew, but perhaps few holidays to the West Country in the 1960s would have been complete without the purchase of a chunky brown glazed mug or lamp base. Somewhat more distinctive than most craft pottery was the output of the Troika Pottery in Cornwall, established in 1963 by the sculptor Lesley Illsley, architect Jan Thompson and potter Benny Sirota. Together they began producing decorative pottery with motifs inspired by artists such as Ben Nicholson and Jean Dubuffet, with pieces usually moulded rather than thrown and featuring heavily incised sgraffito decoration and bright tin glazes sparingly applied. Having established contracts to supply both Heals and Liberty the company enjoyed steady success through the 1960s and 1970s.

To meet the demand for individual and hand-made pottery several major companies established in-house studios to produce experimental and artistic wares, ostensibly separate from day-to-day concerns and pressures of factory mass production. The Poole Pottery in Dorset was a particular exponent of this system and the studio specialised in producing unique or small-run pieces aimed at a discerning clientele. Developed in the Poole Studio by Robert Jefferson and then adapted for mass production, Poole's 1964 Delphis range of wall plates, bowls and vases were hugely popular with the factory struggling to keep pace with demand. With their freely applied abstract patterns in reds, yellows and oranges, Delphis pieces are some of the most instantly recognisable of all 1960s pottery. Bright, acid colours were also a feature of the inexpensive pottery that began to be imported from West Germany later in the decade. Produced by a number of independently operating German factories, these wares were sold widely and typically used heavily applied 'volcanic' type glazes. Monumental in scale, with 60-inch-high floor standing vases a favourite form, these wares have earned the unusual sobriquet 'fat lava' in recent years.

Above: Poole Pottery bowl from the Delphis range.

Below: Cheap and cheerful West German ceramics were a popular purchase – this vase came with chains to allow it to hang on the wall.

GLASS

British glass production at the start of the decade was still largely dominated by traditional cut glass designs for which the industry had a global reputation for excellence. Of the major manufacturers only James Powell and Sons, makers of Whitefriars glass, were active in developing products in contemporary styles, with its ranges, developed in the late 1950s, of thickly walled vases and bowls with controlled bubble decoration. A further range produced by Whitefriars from 1962 matched subtle smoky blue and mauve glass with light symmetrical forms and accorded well with the prevailing trend towards precision and minimalism. Despite Whitefriars' efforts the 'art glass' market in the early 1960s was still dominated by Italian and Scandinavian products. Hand-blown Italian glass, mostly produced by the myriad of small factories based on the Venetian island of Murano, was still marked by its exuberant use of colour; elongated striped decanters, sometimes with delicate filigree or *latticino* inclusions set in the glass, were particularly popular.

Vases by Mona Morales Schildt for Kosta, mid-1960s.

Danish Gulvases designed by Otto Brauer for Holmegaard.

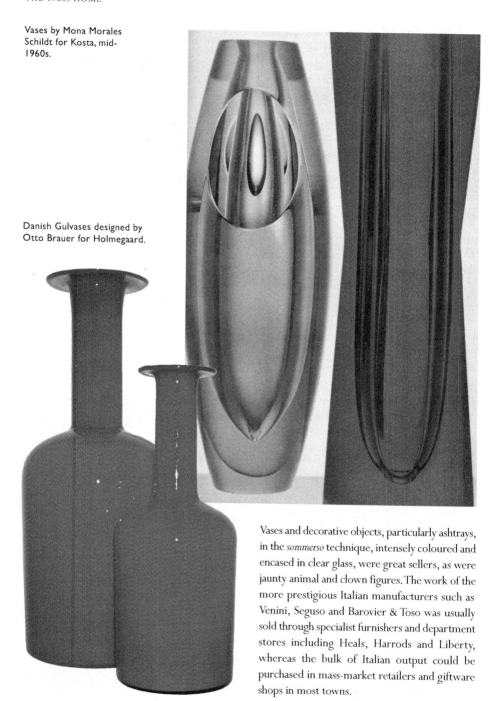

Vases and decorative objects, particularly ashtrays, in the *sommerso* technique, intensely coloured and encased in clear glass, were great sellers, as were jaunty animal and clown figures. The work of the more prestigious Italian manufacturers such as Venini, Seguso and Barovier & Toso was usually sold through specialist furnishers and department stores including Heals, Harrods and Liberty, whereas the bulk of Italian output could be purchased in mass-market retailers and giftware shops in most towns.

Italian glass relied on colour and flair; Scandinavian glass was marked by its cool muted tones and restraint – unlike Italian glass, produced by so many artisan craftsmen, the Scandinavian glass entering Britain was the output of a small number of dominant companies (Kosta and Orrefors in Sweden, Iittala in Finland and Holmegaard in Denmark). By 1960 the organic naturalistic forms redolent of 1950s Scandinavian glass were giving way to more precise geometric shapes. Bestsellers included the Gulvases designed by Otto Brauer for Holmegaard. These bottle-shaped vases with their exaggerated pulled and flattened rims came either in simple thin-walled variants in smoky greys and greens or as more robust types in bright reds, blues and yellows. A slightly later but similar range was christened, appropriately, Carnaby. The Finnish designer Timo Sarpaneva also used bottle and utility shapes for decorative purposes in his elegant 'i' range for Iittala of Finland, and the Swedish designer Mona Morales Schildt developed a layering technique using coloured glass which was then deeply cut to achieve an optical, prism-like effect on otherwise simple shapes. Further into the decade Scandinavian glass began to incorporate texture far more than previously, often by blowing glass into rough formed wooden moulds to produce lively tactile surfaces. Timo Sarpaneva's bark and ice textured vases and range of Festivo candlesticks sold well.

A similar use of texture and surface pattern, although married to a much brighter palette, was employed by the resurgent Whitefriars company with their range of vases designed by Geoffrey Baxter in the mid-1960s. Baxter used materials as diverse as bark, brick and nails in his moulds to achieve a variety of effects. Shapes ranged from simple cylinders to the broken symmetry of the 'drunken bricklayer' vase. The range sold in massive quantities with production only petering out in the 1980s. Other manufacturers attempted to emulate the success of Whitefriars' textured range but never with the aplomb of the original designs.

Glass designed by Geoffrey Baxter for Whitefriars.

Texture in glass – Festivo candlesticks by Timo Sarpaneva for Iittala of Finland.

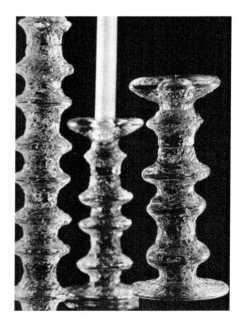

TERENCE CONRAN AND HABITAT

No examination of British homes in the 1960s would be complete without discussing the legacy of designer and entrepreneur Terence Conran, whose first Habitat store opened on London's Fulham Road in 1964. Conran had worked on exhibits for the 1951 Festival of Britain when he was still only twenty, and during the subsequent years of the decade he had designed pottery and fabrics (for Midwinter and David Whitehead respectively) as well as launching a series of restaurants and designing influential shop interiors, notably for Mary Quant in 1957. His company, Conran Design Group, was started in 1956, specialising in interior and exhibition design, furniture and textiles, with a factory in Thetford, Norfolk, set up to make the furniture. Although Conran's furniture in particular sold reasonably well in the contract sector he was, by the early 1960s, becoming increasingly frustrated by the entrenched, old-fashioned practices of traditional furniture retailers whose attitudes he felt thwarted his ambition of providing tasteful, well-made and reasonably priced furniture to a mass market.

Most retailers at the time still sold furniture from samples held in store – with subsequent long delivery times – and often from manufacturers' catalogues alone, and there was little effort made to display furniture in the context of a room setting. Also aware that mainstream retailers were being slow to react to an increasing interest – fostered by the writings of Elizabeth David and others – in French and Mediterranean cooking, Conran arrived at the belief that a shop selling not just furniture but items for every aspect of home life, could be successful.

Interior of the first Habitat store in 1964, with rustic-style chairs and French provincial cookware.

A site was chosen, primarily for its cheapness, on the Fulham Road in West London, then something of a backwater in retailing terms, and Conran and his small team set about selecting items to stock, with Conran naturally providing overall direction and having the ultimate decision on which lines were selected. Cookware was imported from France and included copper and enamel pans alongside unusual items such as pepper-mills, salad bowls, kitchen knives and spaghetti containers, while chairs were brought in from Italy and tableware and other furniture from Scandinavia. These ranges were augmented by Conran's own furniture and fabrics. The overall look – soon to be known universally as 'the Habitat look' – was of lightness, bold colour and rusticity, with a strong emphasis on pale or painted wood, natural materials and simplicity. The shop itself – something of a template for subsequent outlets – had whitewashed brick walls, quarry tiled floors and was lit with spotlights highlighting specific products. Deep shelves were crammed with glasses or pots to give the impression of a shop abundant with stock and mimicked the artlessness of the displays in professional cookware shops that Conran admired. Packaging was also removed so that customers could both see and touch the wares, and likewise the shop was self-service – both novel features at time when supermarkets were still relatively new and most shops kept goods behind counters fronted by sales assistants. Habitat sales assistants were fewer in number but conspicuous perhaps by their Mary Quant clothes and Vidal Sassoon haircuts.

Widely and favourably covered by the national press and attracting a string of celebrity customers – John Lennon amongst them – Habitat captured much of the Zeitgeist about to swing mid-1960s London and in retailing terms at least was an overnight sensation. For many of its early customers – young and affluent though they may have been – the attraction of Habitat went deeper than its novelty. It offered instead the opportunity to buy into a lifestyle stamped with the guarantee of 'good taste' in an unpressurised environment (at a time when many may have lacked the confidence to know what 'good taste' really was). Since the early days of planning the first Habitat, Conran had spoken of his ambition of turning it into a chain of shops and the success of Fulham Road – where they struggled to keep stock levels high enough – made this viable. By 1968 there were four branches, including a new flagship store on London's Tottenham Court Road, the established heart of furniture retailing, and a branch in Manchester, with a total of eighteen shops established by 1974. By this time of course the initial novelty value of Habitat may have worn off, but already its influence on both retailing and interior design had been profound. It both helped usher out the complacent and starchy approach to furniture retailing inherited from the 1950s, and showed also that well made and affordable design need not be the preserve of either solely the rich or of a clique of design-conscious intellectuals.

Habitat promotional photograph from 1967, showing a range of kitchen and tablewares.

KITCHENS AND BATHROOMS

KITCHENS

Throughout the 1950s designers, critics, magazine feature writers and, most of all, manufacturers had consistently promoted the benefits of modern kitchen design. Inevitably, up-to-date kitchens were more likely to be found in new houses and flats in 1960, and indeed this was often a strong selling point for estate agents. Owners of older properties were increasingly investing in either fully-fitted new kitchens too, or at least in some modern labour-saving devices. The ideal, American-style, modern kitchen of the early 1960s was typified by a sleek rectilinear look, with units and work surfaces faced in man-made durable materials such as Formica or Arborite. Handles were usually simple and made of stainless steel or aluminium and often recessed to avoid catching on clothes. Traditional ceramic sinks became rare with the appearance of slimline stainless steel versions with integral draining boards, sometimes enamelled in pastel colours, although metal finishes were both fashionable and suggestive of cleanliness and hygiene. Oven hobs set into worktops first became popular in the 1960s, and a particularly desirable kitchen feature was the raised, eye-level oven with storage units above and below. Freestanding cookers, washing machines and refrigerators were generally clean lined and almost universally finished in white enamel. Dishwashers were still rare and treated with suspicion by many householders, although various counter-top models were available. Tiles, either white or in pale, cool, colours were used for splash areas and floor coverings continued the trend for man-made materials, with linoleum and vinyl coverings generally preferred.

The choice in electrically powered labour-saving kitchen devices increased enormously in the 1960s, their use inhibited only by cost and the general lack of electrical sockets in British kitchens. Electric kettles, toasters, irons and food mixers became far more commonplace than previously, with many new models appearing. The leading industrial designer Kenneth Grange brought the Kenwood Chef food mixer up to date in 1960 and introduced a popular handheld version, the Chefette, in 1966. Drinking coffee was widely

Opposite:
This early-1960s kitchen shows the fashion for clean lines and man-made finishes.

Above: The Kenwood Chef was restyled for a 1960s audience.

Right: Cona coffee maker, 1961.

Flying the flag – Robert Welch's stainless steel designs for Old Hall were a 1960s favourite.

seen as more sophisticated than tea, so coffee makers and machines appeared in increasing numbers. Particularly elegant was the glass and chrome Cona model designed by Abram Games in 1961, still in production today.

The cutlery drawer in a 1960s kitchen was increasingly likely to contain modern cutlery made of stainless steel, which had become far less expensive than in the 1950s and offered many advantages over traditional silver-plate services. Scandinavian stainless steel cutlery with teak or rosewood handles, although elegant, was not always entirely practical on an everyday basis.

From the mid-1960s onwards kitchen design began to move slowly away from the somewhat clinical aesthetic common at the beginning of the decade, with kitchen units more likely to be seen with warmer looking wood or wood-effect facings and with patterned tiles in bold colours becoming popular.

A sense of nostalgia and a wistfulness for the 'traditional' English country kitchen, albeit with modern appliances, was a key aspect of many kitchens by the end of the decade, with pine replacing Formica and other made finishes as the material most in demand. This style was often complemented by boldly patterned blinds and wallpapers with wipe-clean finishes.

BATHROOMS

A common if surprising feature of many interior design and style magazines of the early 1960s is the lack of attention given to bathrooms. Principally this was because the bathroom had traditionally been seen as a purely functional, utilitarian area of the home. Houses with bathrooms were by no means universal in 1960, although they would be, almost, by 1970 and it is perhaps understandable given this that notions of luxury when applied to everyday bathrooms would be slow to form. Many bathrooms were (literally and figuratively) cold; they were harshly lit with linoleum floors, white ceramic tiles and sanitary ware and chrome-plated fittings. The essentials of bathroom design had in many ways changed little since the 1930s, with changes limited to innovations such as close-coupled toilets and cisterns and a general streamlining of suites. As efficient heating found its way into many bathrooms during the course of the decade time spent in the bathroom gradually increased. Coloured suites, typically in pinks and blues but with a palette broadening to encompass greens and dark browns by the mid- to late-1960s were gradually introduced to the market. These could be matched to taps and fittings enamelled in complementing colours. Tiles likewise were more likely to be coloured or patterned – if they were indeed retained at all, as a fondness for tongue and groove pine panelling was evident by the mid-1960s. Few householders would have countenanced carpeting in bathrooms during the 1950s or before, but yet again these became increasingly used as waterproof varieties became widely available. Many older

Stainless steel salad servers with rosewood handles – Lundtofte Denmark, mid-1960s.

By the late 1960s
bathrooms were
more informal –
here a Victorian
roll top bath has
been given a
contemporary
look.

houses had larger bathrooms which had been converted from bedrooms and
these in particular lent themselves to revivalist styles, with the previously
unloved 'claw' footed roll-top baths of the Victorian era becoming especially
valued.

Early-1960s
bathrooms were
often austere.

CONCLUSION

DESIGN and decorative styles of the 1960s enjoyed a somewhat equivocal reputation for many years after the close of the decade. The historicist styles in evidence by the end of the 1960s would retain their hold on British homes for many years and whilst the fashions, films and, most of all, popular music of the 1960s would be celebrated widely, its domestic design would be viewed with bemusement at best. For many the popular image of 1960s home design was of ephemerality and excess, of plastic or paper chairs and lurid carpets and wallpaper. That the plastic and paper chairs are now likely only to be seen in museums perhaps illustrates best how little impact they had on everyday homes at the time. Whilst 1960s domestic design may have been met with bewilderment its housing and architecture often inspired hostility, its buildings seen as monuments to the hubris of architects and planners and its successes overwhelmed by its spectacular failures. Nevertheless, 1960s architecture has undergone a generally more sympathetic, if tentative, re-appraisal in recent years than many may have once have thought possible. Enthusiasm for its domestic design has on the other hand burgeoned since the 1990s – initially as enthusiasts sought out original furniture, pottery and glass from the era and then later as a groundswell of manufacturers reissued furniture designs from the 1960s to a receptive market. As mid-century-inspired designs and idioms have filtered increasingly into the mass market during the twenty-first century the legacy of the 1960s is more apparent in British homes than ever before.

The old and the new – an eighteenth-century French armoire and a contemporary tulip table – meet in this late 1960s day room.

INDEX